have needed to stay at the school because of the distance and there was no money for that. But I was a very determined person and was totally focussed on going to school and university. I say I was determined, but maybe it was more that I was a fighter, a survivor.

When I was fourteen years old, I went to the school in Arad and asked to speak to the director. I think she might have been surprised at my visit.

'Here I am,' I said. 'I have come to take the school's entrance exam. But, if I pass the exam, I will need an allowance to keep me while I am here. I am very poor and cannot survive without an allowance.'

'You are very courageous for a fourteen-year-old,' the director replied. 'Take the exam and let's see how you get on.'

I sat the exam and passed. Once again I went to see the director.

'This is my result,' I said. 'I have come fifth on the list. Now can I have an allowance to become a boarding pupil at your school?'

She was probably surprised at how well I had done.

'I think so,' she said.

The director argued my case and said that because I had come in very good time I should get a full allowance, meaning all my expenses would be paid. That year there was a system in place for reducing the costs for pupils from poor families, and there were some really poor families in Romania then. It was unusual for a pupil of my age to get a full allowance at that school. I could never have gone there without it.

HOME VERSUS SCHOOL

My father was a Christian who learned to read through reading the Bible. When I was young, I didn't realise what hard work that must have been and that, although he was not educated, he must have been very clever. My mother was not educated either.

Dad read Bible stories to me and my brother. I remember him trying to teach me about Daniel and the lions' den. It was an interesting story, but I didn't understand that it also had a meaning. I didn't take any message from it although Dad tried to tell it in a way to give me the message. Part of me didn't want to understand. You see, I admired my school teachers because they were educated. I looked up to them. At that time in Romania we were brainwashed at school. We were taught that there was no God. Because my teachers were educated and Dad was not, I thought that they must be right. He said that God existed; my teachers said he did not, therefore I decided there was no god.

VIO JORZA

I was brought up in a village near Arad in Romania. We were a poor family living in a poor village. My parents didn't have enough money to let me go to high school in Arad. I would

THE MISSING PIECE

The Life Story of Vio Jorza

Edited by Irene Howat

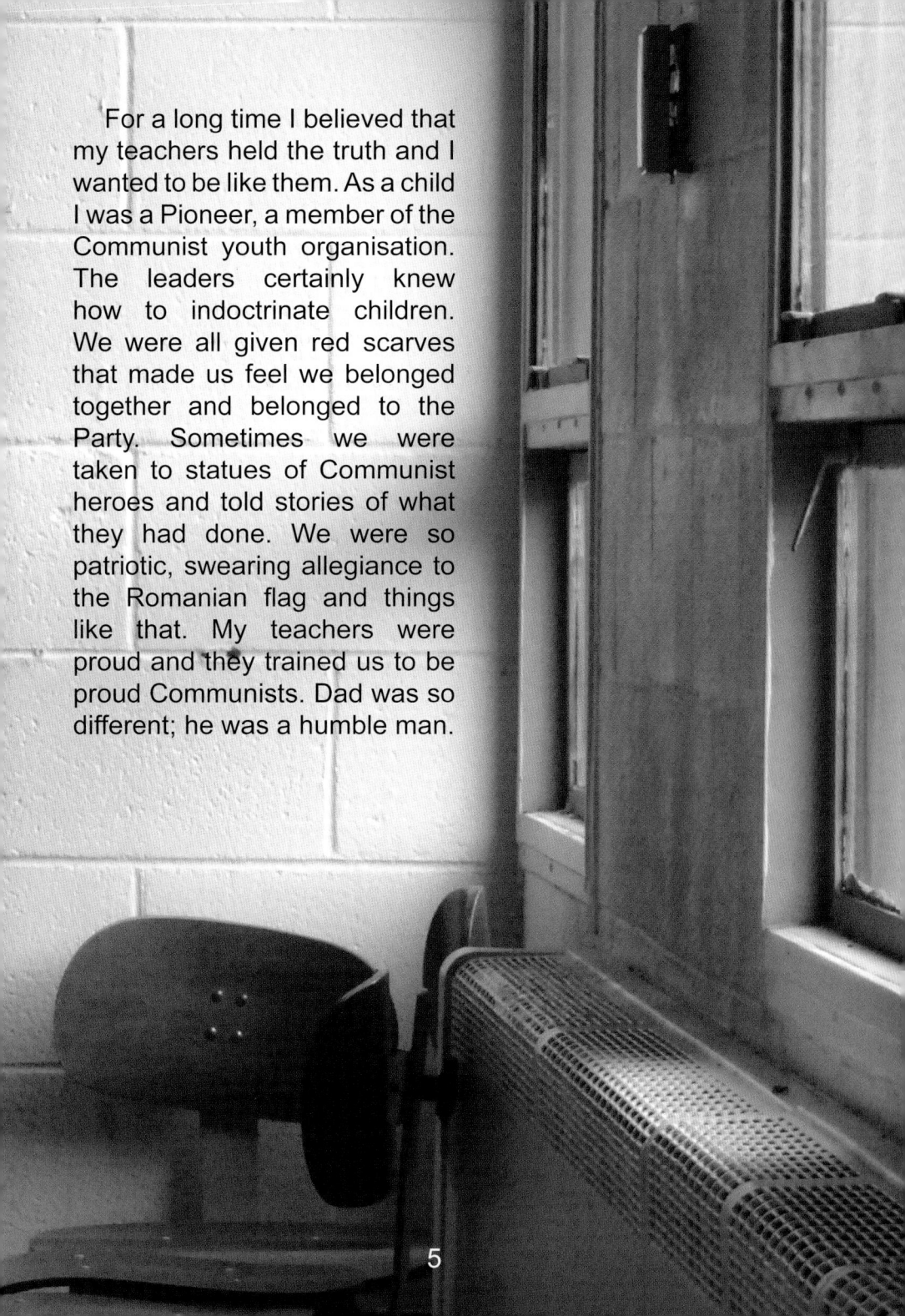

For a long time I believed that my teachers held the truth and I wanted to be like them. As a child I was a Pioneer, a member of the Communist youth organisation. The leaders certainly knew how to indoctrinate children. We were all given red scarves that made us feel we belonged together and belonged to the Party. Sometimes we were taken to statues of Communist heroes and told stories of what they had done. We were so patriotic, swearing allegiance to the Romanian flag and things like that. My teachers were proud and they trained us to be proud Communists. Dad was so different; he was a humble man.

DAD'S STORY

Dad farmed a small piece of land. He had been a soldier in the Second World War. For a time he was under Russians and for a time under Germans. I remember him telling me how he became a Christian.

'We were in the trenches,' he told me, 'just waiting to be attacked. For the first time in my life I prayed to God. And my prayer was, "If you are God, you will spare my life and let me go back to my children and I will trust you."'

He already had children then although my brother and I had not yet been born.

After that battle, my father had to run for his life; they all had to run for their lives. Later, when he saw his long coat, there were bullet holes in it. His legs were not hurt although he was shot at as he ran. Dad was alive and he saw God. The bullet holes in the coat were a testimony to God protecting not only his legs, but his life. When he saw God, Dad said, 'You must be God and you spared my life.' I can't explain what happened to Dad. I'm just telling what he told me.

Soon after my father was back in our village, an itinerant missionary came and, when he and Dad talked, my father embraced the Christian faith. That day he told the missionary, 'I want to have more children and to give them to the Lord.'

REBELLIOUS

It must have been hard for Dad because my brother and I were prayed for since before we were born and when we grew older we did not believe in God. In fact, I was very rebellious. One memory especially fills me with shame. I remember asking my father, 'How are we blessed? I don't see any blessing here. We are the poorest in the village and you came back from the war with so many wounds.' One of Dad's lungs had been damaged and he used to cough up blood. It was such a difficult time for our family. Mum used to tell us to be good, to be quiet and not to annoy Dad because he might die. 'Tell me one blessing,' I demanded. Dad said, 'My children, you are my blessings and you are very smart.'

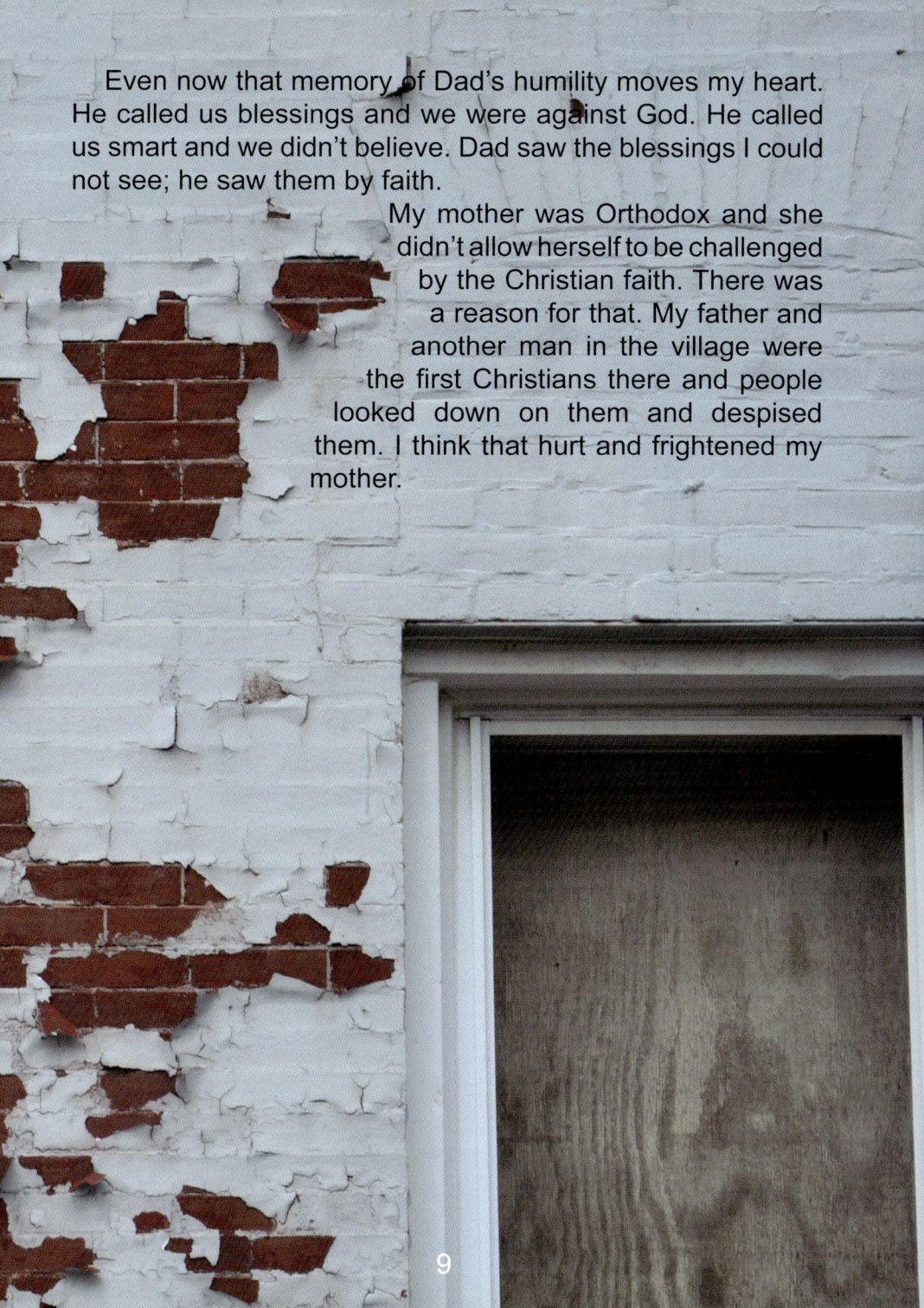

Even now that memory of Dad's humility moves my heart. He called us blessings and we were against God. He called us smart and we didn't believe. Dad saw the blessings I could not see; he saw them by faith.

My mother was Orthodox and she didn't allow herself to be challenged by the Christian faith. There was a reason for that. My father and another man in the village were the first Christians there and people looked down on them and despised them. I think that hurt and frightened my mother.

SEARCHING OR BELIEVING

Mum saw and heard Dad trying to teach us. But my father didn't know how to teach. He used to tell us that we just had to believe rather than search, that 'searching' was what we were taught to do in school. Our teachers instructed us to search ideas, not just believe what we were told. But the truth is that they were indoctrinating us, forcing us to accept their thinking and making it sound silly to believe what our parents said. They were lying to us. Truth was the opposite of what they said. The Bible tells us to search everything and to take what is good. Even now the memory of my father is so vivid. When people say 'the God of Abraham, Isaac and Jacob,' I say, 'the God of my father.'

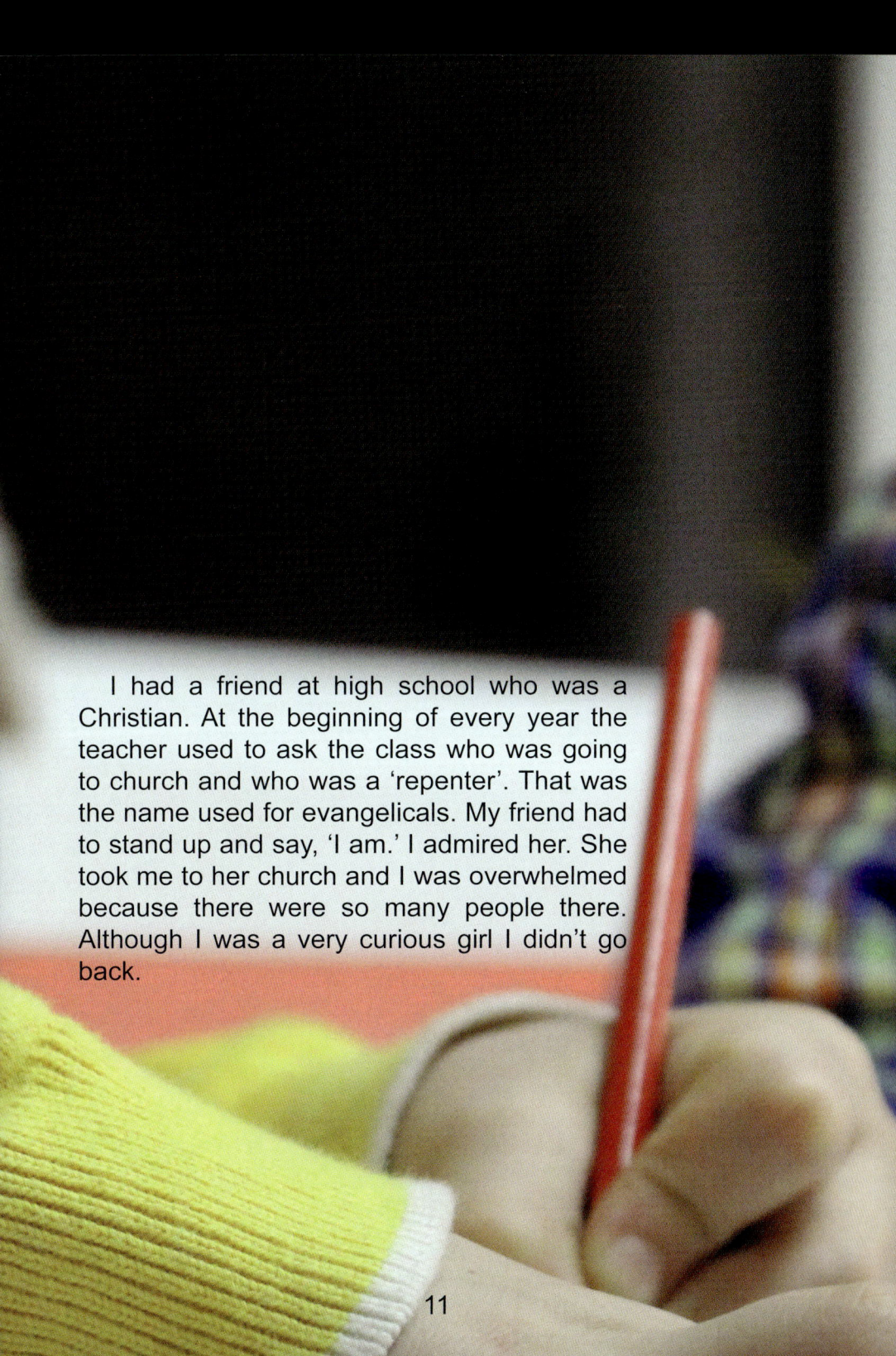

I had a friend at high school who was a Christian. At the beginning of every year the teacher used to ask the class who was going to church and who was a 'repenter'. That was the name used for evangelicals. My friend had to stand up and say, 'I am.' I admired her. She took me to her church and I was overwhelmed because there were so many people there. Although I was a very curious girl I didn't go back.

THE MISSING PIECE

People said I was smart and I was often first in the class. What they didn't know was that I was determined to learn and become rich, to get away from our grinding poverty. But, when I left school, I hit the same old problem again, there was no money for me to go to university. Mum had died and I stayed with my sister in Arad. There was a children's home across the road and I went there to speak to the director. After I told her about my life, and that I loved children and needed to work to get through university, she said she'd take me on trial for a few days. I worked hard and she employed me. Starting at the lowest level, I cared for children and went to university at the same time. Later, I became a teacher and after that a speech therapist in the same institution. I was at the children's home for many years.

I had thought that university would fulfil my life, but it was so empty. Something was missing. Then I met a young man who played in the Philharmonic orchestra in Arad. We were married and I thought this would fill my life. But after a year, when I was in my third year at university, I discovered he was homosexual. In Romania that was a criminal offence and he could have been put in prison. I did not want that. I was crushed in every area of my life when we split up and then divorced.

On Christmas Day 1986 I was a very sad person. Looking out of the window of my sister's home I could see Speranța Church and watched as many people went in. They all looked so happy and I wondered why. In desperation I decided to go to church, but the building was so full I couldn't find a seat. As people knew I was a stranger, they made a place for me at the front. I felt so ashamed and couldn't even raise my eyes when the sermon started. It was about Jesus, how he came into the world.

I felt so guilty that I'd wasted my life by not believing what my father had said. Crying tears of shame and joy at the same time, I discovered that there is a God, that there was a way out of my misery and desperation. From that time I went to church, turned to God and started reading the Bible. It was such a joy to discover the truth of it.

MAKE SOMETHING BEAUTIFUL

As I had never read the Bible before, it was a new world opening to me. Such joy filled my heart and it was the beginning of my new life. I remember praying, 'Lord, you are God. You have power. You see my life is broken. (I pictured a broken vase.) You can take it. You can make something for your glory. I promise I will obey you even when I don't understand.' I challenged God to make something beautiful from my life, promising I would obey him.

Before long I wanted to be baptised, but the orphanage was near the church and that was a problem for me. I prayed, 'Oh Lord, all my colleagues will see me here when I get baptised and they will laugh and look down on me.' A day or two before my baptism the orphanage was closed because of an epidemic. It was closed to disinfect the building and nobody was there. That day eighty-five people were baptised as there was revival in Romania then.

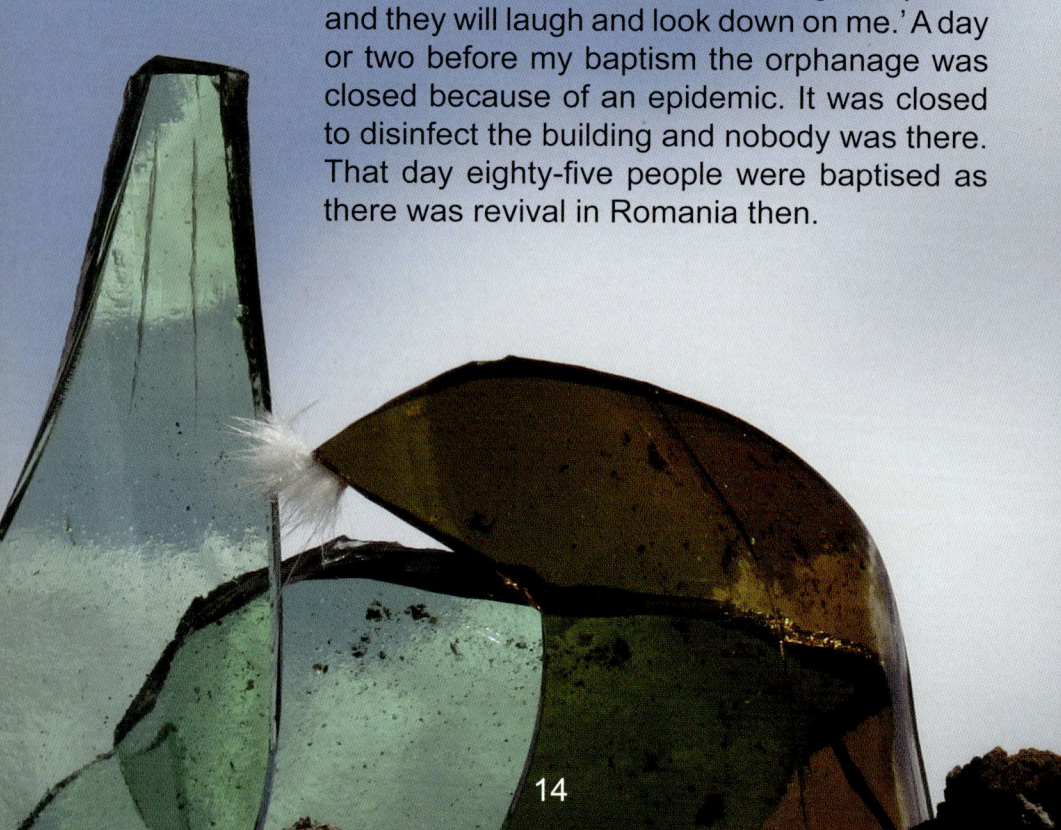

UNDERGROUND MINISTRY

After I gave my testimony in front of the church, a lady working in the Sunday school came straight up to me. She said, 'I feel you should work in Sunday school. We need people there and you are the right person.' Because God gave me a love for boys and girls, I knew from the beginning that the call of my life was to work with children. We had regular checks from the government because it was against the law to teach children about Christianity. They said we could sing with them, but not teach the Bible. We were doing an underground ministry and, when they came to check, we just stopped what we were teaching and started singing.

I remember one Easter day we had a lesson about Jesus on the cross on flannel boards. A lady came rushing in and said, 'Gather everything. The checking is here.'

We had to take everything down and start singing! I also began to organise camps for children away from the town, in secret, in hiding. The other lady teacher lost her job because she gave someone Christian literature. I didn't lose my job because nobody wanted to work in the orphanage. It was a humble job.

A TRAGIC PLACE

Working in the orphanage was very difficult. We had four dorms with twenty children in each. As it was usually one nurse and one carer for twenty children, we hardly managed to change their nappies, feed them and then start again. There was no time to cuddle the children, no time to work with them. As we didn't have carpets to put them on, they couldn't walk, they couldn't move anywhere. They were in beds with no toys, with no stimulation.

Years later, when I was a speech therapist, there was a doctor who was a Christian. The pair of us prayed that the Lord would change life for the children in the orphanage. We believed that Communism would stay for ever; we couldn't imagine it collapsing. But we prayed that the Lord would change things and give us the opportunity to do something for these children, to really help them. When the revolution came, that building was taken over by an English believer and it became a Christian home for a time.

REVOLUTION!

In December 1989, I heard that something was happening in Arad and went with others to see what it was. I saw with my own eyes tanks and soldiers and massive crowds of people coming from factories. And I cried when youngsters going from factories walked hand in hand toward the tanks, thinking they would all die. I prayed that the Lord would turn things when the mass of people arrived at the tanks. One of the youngsters had flowers and climbed on a tank and gave the flowers to the soldiers. Perhaps he said that we were all Romanians and wanted peace. Nothing happened. No cruelty. No fires.

Somebody came and called for the people's attention and then asked us to pray The Lord's Prayer. Everything stopped and everyone knelt down in front of the town council to pray. Pastors climbed on to a platform made especially for them, made spontaneously, and they preached that God exists. It was overwhelming. To say God exists while Ceausescu was still living! That could have cost lives. God's hand was over us because nobody died that day. That was the first day of the revolution in Arad. After the revolution a new world opened.

How can I sum up my story? I think God answered my father's prayers. He put all the pieces of my life together and it's great to be able to serve such a wonderful God. He fills my life, and not only mine, for he also allows me to share the good news that Jesus is the only Saviour with so many others. It's wonderful. He is wonderful!

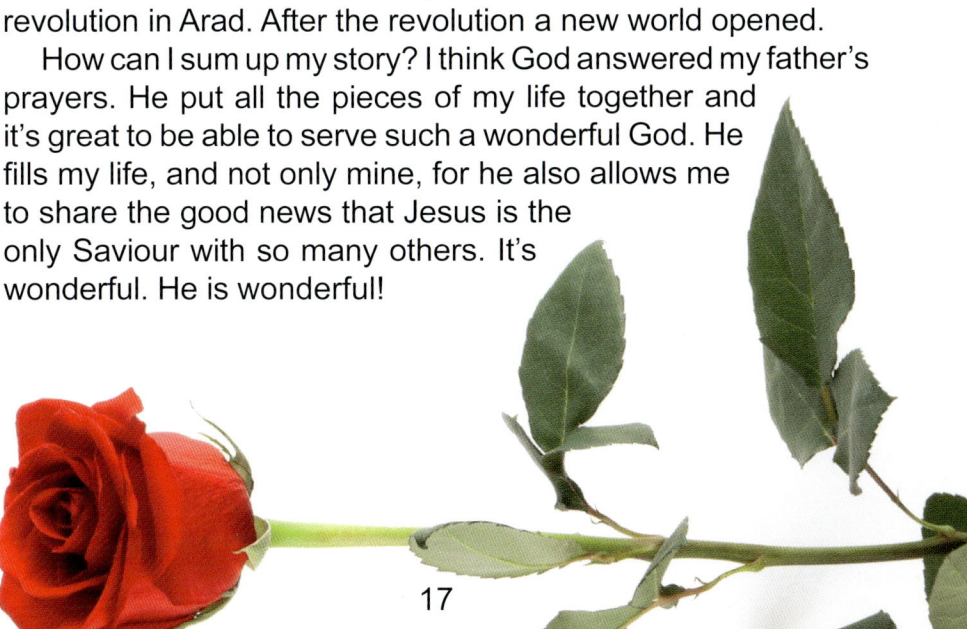

MATTHEW 6:5-15
THE LORD'S PRAYER

[5] "And when you pray, you must not be like the hypocrites. For they love to stand and pray in the synagogues and at the street corners, that they may be seen by others. Truly, I say to you, they have received their reward. [6] But when you pray, go into your room and shut the door and pray to your Father who is in secret. And your Father who sees in secret will reward you.

[7] "And when you pray, do not heap up empty phrases as the Gentiles do, for they think that they will be heard for their many words. [8] Do not be like them, for your Father knows what you need before you ask him. [9] Pray then like this:

"Our Father in heaven, hallowed be your name.[10] Your kingdom come, your will be done, on earth as it is in heaven.

[11] Give us this day our daily bread, [12] and forgive us our debts, as we also have forgiven our debtors.[13] And lead us not into temptation,but deliver us from evil. [14] For if you forgive others their trespasses, your heavenly Father will also forgive you, [15] but if you do not forgive others their trespasses, neither will your Father forgive your trespasses.

Dear friend,

You have heard my life story. Now you might wonder how your life will be and where it will lead. My father was praying for me – not just for a year or two, but for almost thirty. And God answered his prayers.

God is our Father in heaven. Yes, he is yours too! You can always talk to him, you can pray to him. You will discover, as I did once, that you are not alone, even if it sometimes feels like it. He can fix any life, even yours. Not only that, but he has the power to turn the bad things in your life into something good. He can give you joy and fulfilment. Come to him now. Do not wait!

BLYTHSWOOD CARE

Blythswood Care provides practical help, love and support for those in need. Whether through filled shoeboxes at Christmas, relief and development aid or social projects for young and old, Blythswood brings hope to families in Europe, Africa and Asia. For every £1 donated, Blythswood delivers more than £5 worth of grass roots aid. With the support of ordinary people like you, Blythswood achieves EXTRAORDINARY transformations and provides loving care for body and soul.

Head Office:
Highland Deephaven, Evanton, Ross-shire, Scotland, IV16 9XJ
email: info@blythswood.org

Published in 2016
by
Christian Focus Publications, Geanies House,
Fearn, Ross-shire, IV20 1TW, Scotland, U.K.
www.christianfocus.com
Text by Irene Howat
Cover design by Daniel van Straaten
Printed and bound in China

Pictures on page 2 and 22 - author's own
Picture on page 6 was taken by the Finnish Army and is in the public domain.
Pictures on pages 3, 4-5, 8-9, 10-11, 13, 14-15, 16, 17, 19 are all free images from Morguefile.com free stock.